The Hilla-Crimes Coloring Book

The Hilarious Crimes of Hillary Rodham Clinton!

by Leslie Tran

The Hilla-Crimes Coloring Book:
The Hilarious Crimes of Hillary Rodham Clinton!

Copyright © 2016 by Leslie Tran

Cover and Illustrations by: Leslie Tran

ISBN-13: 978-0692751848
ISBN-10: 069275184X

Give feedback on the book at:
Mr.LeslieTran@gmail.com

Join me on:
Twitter: @MrLeslieTran
Facebook: fb.com/MrLeslieTran
Tumblr: MrLeslieTran.tumblr.com
Instagram: instagram.com/MrLeslieTran

Printed in U.S.A

The following images were created using eye witness accounts of the many crimes of Hillary Rodham Clinton:

The Amsterdam heist

The bloodbath in the ruins of Machu Picchu

The drunken crash in Putin's stash

Consuming hundreds of taxpayer dollars in the form of fancy "money sandwiches"

Literally hundreds of
DUIs

6' 0"

5' 6"

5' 0"

4' 6"

4' 0"

3' 6"

3' 0"

Discharging unregistered firearms

Provocative hand
gestures:
"Suck my pussy,
CNN!"

Killing of England's mascot: the White Rabbit

Watches
"The Adventures of Mary-Kate & Ashley" detective movies on Netflix over and over and over again

FACT: If you got that grass, Hillary's got that ass

Personally killed 10 baby highland gorillas for a fur coat

Used taxpayer dollars to create a tongue kissing sex clone

Destroyed EMAIL!

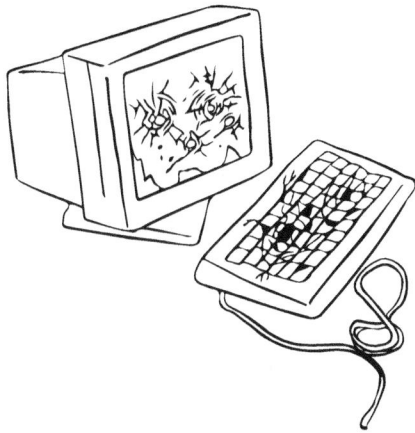

Hillary is known to fake an interest in organized sports

Regularly shows up drunk at the Smithsonian Zoo to taunt the pandas

Famously re-trained President Bill Clinton on the White House Lawn

Appeared in several erotic lesbian films, but later refused to sign the talent release forms

Forced mentally retarded Alaskan Governor Sarah Palin into an oil pit battle

Known to flash her "kitty" at FOX NEWS reporters

Hillary Rodham Clinton is a bigger badass than you :)

Check out the entire series!

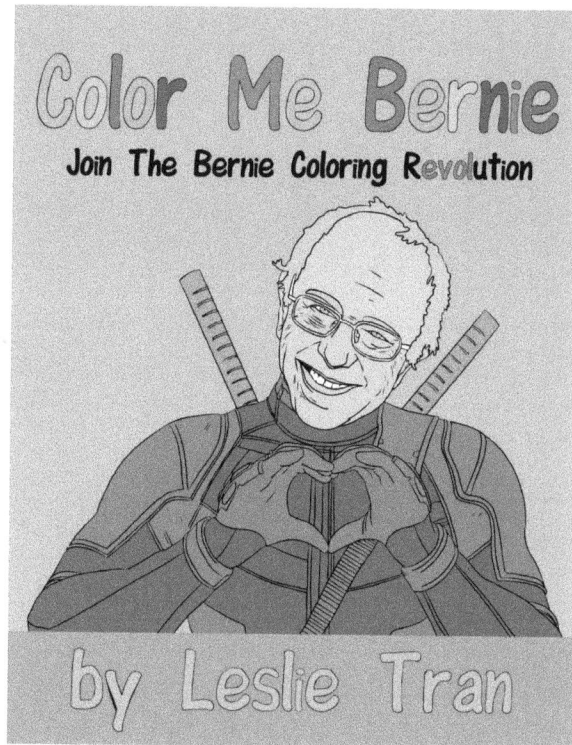

**Available Now on
Createspace, Amazon & Barnes & Noble**

Post-Presidency
Obama

**Working title
and cover**

Hillary vs Trump

**Working title
and cover**

Available Very Soon

Available Very Soon